Original title:
Rising with Hope

Copyright © 2024 Swan Charm
All rights reserved.

Author: Liina Liblikas
ISBN HARDBACK: 978-9916-89-643-3
ISBN PAPERBACK: 978-9916-89-644-0
ISBN EBOOK: 978-9916-89-645-7

Lifted by Dreams

In the quiet night's embrace,
Whispers of hope dance and trace.
Stars ignite the endless sky,
Carrying wishes that float high.

In gardens where visions bloom,
We find light dispelling gloom.
Each heartbeat speaks of a flight,
An ascent into the bright.

Horizons of Renewal

Beyond the hills, the dawn awakes,
With every breath, a promise breaks.
Rivers flow with stories true,
Carving paths for me and you.

In every shadow lies a spark,
Guiding dreams through the dark.
Hands together, we will rise,
Chasing gold-lit morning skies.

A New Day's Promise

Fingers trace the golden light,
Embracing change with all our might.
The horizon calls, a gentle song,
Believing together, we belong.

Sunrise paints the world anew,
With hope so bright, we start to pursue.
Each moment holds a chance to grow,
In the warmth, our spirits flow.

Soaring Spirits

Wings unfurl in the morning air,
With every heartbeat, dreams declare.
Echoes of laughter fill the skies,
As we learn to rise and rise.

Adventures wait on every breeze,
Carried forth with grace and ease.
In unity, we find our way,
Soaring spirits greet the day.

The Climb Towards Tomorrow

In the dawn's gentle light, we rise,
Step by step, reaching for the skies.
With hope in our hearts, we journey on,
Through trials and fears, till the night is gone.

Each rock we climb, strengthens our will,
With every breath, silence the chill.
We forge ahead, hand in hand,
Together, we'll make our final stand.

The view from the top, oh what a sight,
Mountains behind, future so bright.
With dreams as our guide, we won't fall,
The climb towards tomorrow, it's worth it all.

Through valleys deep, and shadows long,
We find our courage, we grow strong.
With every stumble, we rise anew,
Each step taken, leads us to truth.

So let us climb, with spirits high,
Fear not the clouds, nor the sky.
For in our hearts, the fire will glow,
Together we thrive, come join the show.

A Tidal Wave of Positivity

Riding the waves of bright delight,
Every smile shines, a guiding light.
Moments shared, we build our dreams,
In this ocean, nothing's as it seems.

With laughter echoing through the air,
We spread love, it's everywhere.
Hand in hand, we dance and sway,
In a tidal wave, we find our way.

Together we rise, like the sun at dawn,
Wiping out fears, like dew on the lawn.
With hearts wide open, we receive,
In this joyful realm, we truly believe.

Life's a journey, let's embrace each turn,
From storms that clash, to fires that burn.
As waves of kindness crash and flow,
A tidal wave of positivity, let's grow.

So come along, let your spirit fly,
On this wave of joy, we'll soar high.
In the ocean of hope, we'll brightly shine,
Together forever, your heart with mine.

Beyond the Twilight

Beneath the fading light,
Whispers of night unfold,
Dreams take flight with grace,
In shadows, secrets told.

Stars begin to shimmer,
Painting the sky with hope,
The world holds its breath tight,
In darkness, we elope.

Ghosts of day retreat slow,
As constellations play,
The moon sings soft lullabies,
Guiding the lost on their way.

In this silent embrace,
Time gently flows away,
Memories drift like clouds,
As night becomes the day.

Beyond the twilight's grace,
New journeys start to call,
With courage in our hearts,
We rise, and never fall.

The Symphony of Renewal

In spring's gentle whisper,
Life begins to bloom anew,
Colors dance in the breeze,
Painting earth's canvas true.

Raindrops kiss thirsty soil,
Nature sings in rich refrain,
Every seed a promise,
Of joy from heartache's pain.

Birds return from their travels,
With melodies on the air,
Hope floats on their wings,
Spreading love everywhere.

As sunlight breaks the shadows,
The world feels alive once more,
Awakening our spirits,
To dreams we can't ignore.

A symphony of triumph,
In harmony, we stand tall,
Together we embrace change,
In unity, we will not fall.

Awakening Hearts

Silent whispers in the dawn,
Calls that stir the sleeping soul,
In the hush of morning light,
We begin to feel whole.

With each breath, awaken dreams,
Woven in the fabric of time,
Hearts that yearn and hearts that seek,
In rhythm, hearts will rhyme.

Footsteps echo on the path,
Explorers of our inner streams,
Finding strength in vulnerability,
And courage in our dreams.

Together we ignite the fire,
A blaze of purpose intertwined,
As we dance to life's great melody,
In love, we're ever aligned.

Awakening hearts in passion,
Tender and fiercely alive,
With faith, we'll forge our stories,
In truth, we will survive.

Forwards into the Dawn

With the rising sun ahead,
We step beyond our fears,
In each golden ray we trust,
Wiping away our tears.

The past a distant echo,
Fading with the night's embrace,
Today we claim our journey,
With fire, passion, and grace.

Each footfall strong and steady,
Forging paths through the pine,
Together we'll reach the summit,
With hearts that brightly shine.

The horizon calls our name,
A canvas vast and wide,
Forwards into the dawn,
With hope as our guide.

So hand in hand, we'll venture,
Into the unknown we stride,
Forwards into the dawn,
With love as our steady tide.

The Light After the Rain

The clouds begin to part,
A gentle sun breaks through,
Raindrops on leaves glisten,
Each spark a drop of dew.

A rainbow stretches wide,
Colors burst in the sky,
Hope is painted bright,
As storms slowly say goodbye.

Puddles shimmer like glass,
Reflecting joy anew,
Nature breathes a sigh,
As skies turn fresh and blue.

Life resumes its dance,
With whispers of the breeze,
In the heart of spring,
The world feels at ease.

So let the rain cleanse all,
And wash away our fears,
For after every storm,
The light brings happy tears.

Coursing Streams of Inspiration

Ideas flow like rivers,
In currents swift and strong,
They carve through rocky paths,
Where dreams and hopes belong.

From mountain tops they tumble,
In waterfalls of thought,
Each drop a spark of wisdom,
In the depths of what is sought.

With twists and turns they wander,
Through valleys rich with lore,
Every bend reveals a tale,
That takes us to the shore.

The echoes of their journey,
Whisper into our hearts,
Reminding us of beauty,
In all our separate arts.

So let the waters guide us,
As we chase the written word,
For inspiration flows freely,
When our souls are gently stirred.

An Uplifted Spirit

With every breath we take,
There's power in our stride,
A whisper of the heart,
That lifts us from inside.

The weight of doubts dissolves,
Like fog in morning light,
As laughter paints the sky,
In colors pure and bright.

We stand upon the peaks,
With arms spread open wide,
Reaching for the heavens,
Embracing life's sweet ride.

Through valleys of despair,
We find our strength once more,
With hope as our companion,
We rise, we soar, we explore.

So dance upon the wind,
With joy that knows no end,
For every spirit lifted,
Will always find a friend.

Illuminated Pathways

In shadows deep and dark,
The light begins to glow,
A path of purest gold,
Inviting us to go.

With lanterns bright and warm,
We step with hearts aglow,
Each stride a whispered promise,
Of places yet to know.

The moonbeams guide our journey,
Through forests lush and free,
Illuminated pathways,
Lead us to destiny.

In every twist and turn,
Magic weaves its thread,
As footprints leave their stories,
Wherever we are led.

So follow where it takes you,
With courage, take a chance,
For in the light of guidance,
We learn, we grow, we dance.

The Lifting of Clouds

In the quiet morn, the mist does lift,
Revealing a world, a gentle gift.
Sunbeams dance on dewy grass,
Nature sighs, as shadows pass.

A canvas bright, the skies receive,
Colors bloom, as hearts believe.
Hope is born with every ray,
A promise bright for a new day.

Birds take flight, in joyous song,
Each note proclaiming where they belong.
Above the heights, they soar and glide,
On whispers soft, the winds they ride.

Mountains stand, their peaks in view,
Guardians brave, in shades of blue.
They watch the world, both calm and wild,
In every heart, the spirit smiled.

As clouds disperse, a vision clear,
Life unfolds, and peace draws near.
In every corner, love abounds,
In the blessing of the lifting clouds.

Awakening Dawn

The darkness fades; the light breaks through,
A gentle touch of morning dew.
Birds begin their heartfelt call,
To celebrate the rise of all.

The world stirs in soft embrace,
Sunshine paints each hidden place.
A canvas brushed with golden hues,
Awakens dreams and ancient views.

Flowers lift their heads so bright,
Greeting warmth, embracing light.
Whispers of the day unfold,
In nature's arms, a tale retold.

Gentle breezes kiss the air,
Inviting peace beyond compare.
Where hands reach out, and smiles abound,
In the gentle glow of awakening dawn.

With every heartbeat, life reclaims,
The beauty found in morning's flames.
A serenade to those who yearn,
For the magic of the dawn's return.

Ascending with Light

In the still of night, dreams take flight,
As stars align, the soul feels light.
Beyond the shadows, hope takes hold,
A journey bright, a tale retold.

With every step, the heart ignites,
Chasing the warmth of wondrous sights.
Each dawn reveals a path anew,
Guided by light, in skies so blue.

Mountains rise, and valleys call,
Embracing all, both great and small.
Adventure waits on wings of grace,
With light to guide, to interlace.

In silence strong, we find our way,
Through countless nights, to greet the day.
Each moment fresh, like lifted wings,
In the dance of life, our spirit sings.

Ascending high, we touch the skies,
With every breath, our spirit flies.
Together bound, our hearts unite,
In harmony, ascending with light.

Embracing Tomorrow

With every dawn, a chance to grow,
To let the past fade, to let it go.
In hope we stride, our dreams held tight,
Embracing all, with hearts alight.

The future waits, a canvas wide,
With strokes of joy, we cast aside.
Each moment cherished, each laugh we share,
In the beauty of a world laid bare.

Together we rise, with hands entwined,
Creating paths, and hearts aligned.
Through every struggle, love endures,
A promise made, in faith, ensures.

With courage strong, we face the storm,
Finding strength in every form.
In unity, we find our way,
Determined hearts, come what may.

So here we stand, in time's embrace,
With open arms, we find our place.
Together we build, beneath the sky,
Embracing tomorrow, you and I.

New Beginnings Unfurled

A seed breaks the ground below,
Soft whispers of springtime grow.
The sun paints paths on dewy grass,
Hope awakens, shadows pass.

Fresh buds kiss the morning air,
Joy dances without a care.
Nature unfolds her tapestry,
Life's promise blooms, wild and free.

Birds chirp with a sweet refrain,
Each note echoes, love's domain.
New dreams rise with the dawn's light,
Together we embrace the bright.

The past lightly fades away,
As courage leads the heart to play.
With every step, a chance to find,
New beginnings, intertwined.

Let the journey start anew,
With open heart, and skies so blue.
In every moment, joy will weave,
A story that the soul believes.

Above the Deepening Night

Stars ripple in the velvet sky,
Whispers of dreams that never die.
Moonlight dances on silver streams,
Casting shadows where spirit gleams.

A hush settles on the world below,
Secrets in the night begin to flow.
The air, thick with tales untold,
Guided by starlight, brave and bold.

Crickets sing a lullaby sweet,
Nature's serenade, a healing beat.
In the quiet, we find our peace,
As worries fade and sorrows cease.

Above the deepening night so vast,
Flickering hopes in shadows cast.
With every breath, the heart takes flight,
Embracing the magic of the night.

In the stillness, we find our way,
Under celestial watch, we sway.
Finding solace in starry grace,
A journey woven in time and space.

Lanterns in the Fog

Beneath the veil of misty shrouds,
Lanterns flicker, drawing crowds.
A soft glow that guides the way,
Through hidden paths where shadows play.

Each light tells a tale of hope,
In the darkness, we learn to cope.
The fog wraps tightly, whispers near,
But lanterns shine, and hearts feel clear.

As footsteps carry us along,
We find the rhythm of our song.
In unity, our spirits rise,
Together we dance beneath the skies.

The night is deep, but bright with dreams,
Each lantern brightens, or so it seems.
As flickers join to make a line,
In the fog, our spirits entwine.

With every step, we brave the night,
Guided by lanterns, soft and bright.
A journey shared, a path we make,
Together, stronger, for friendship's sake.

A Song of Renewal

In tides of change, we find our voice,
A symphony that makes us rejoice.
Each note a whisper, soft and clear,
In the dance of life, we draw near.

Seasons shift and days unfold,
Stories of courage, brave and bold.
With every sunrise, new chances bloom,
A song of renewal, dispelling gloom.

Tethered to dreams, we rise above,
Moments crafted with strength and love.
With every heartbeat, we write our song,
Reminding us where we belong.

In harmony, our hearts unite,
Together, we embrace the light.
With every note, we learn to grow,
A melody that softly flows.

So raise your voice, let it be heard,
In the chorus of life, every word.
With open arms, we face the new,
In this song of renewal, we break through.

The Light That Follows

In shadows deep, a whisper calls,
A beacon shines as darkness falls.
With gentle warmth, it guides the way,
To brighter realms where dreams can play.

Each step we take, the bonds we weave,
In trust and love, we dare believe.
The light that follows, soft and true,
Illuminates the path anew.

Through winding roads and trials faced,
The heart learns strength, and hope is chased.
For with each dawn, the shadows flee,
Revealing all that's meant to be.

Together we rise, hand in hand,
In every heartbeat, we will stand.
The light that follows, steady glow,
Will lead us where our spirits flow.

So let the daybreak's promise shine,
In every moment, love divine.
Through every challenge, we will find,
The light that follows, unconfined.

Veils of Hope Unfurled

Beneath the surface, dreams take flight,
In whispered prayers, we search for light.
Veils of hope begin to sway,
Unfurled with grace, they greet the day.

In gardens where the wildflowers bloom,
We find the strength to rise from gloom.
Each petal tells of journeys past,
Resilience born, our hearts amassed.

With every breath, a promise grows,
In silent moments, courage flows.
Veils of hope, both soft and bright,
Embrace the darkness, birth the light.

Through valleys deep, our spirits soar,
In unity, we seek for more.
Together we'll ignite the fire,
Veils of hope, our true desire.

For every story that we share,
Awakens dreams; we learn to care.
With open hearts, we take our stand,
Veils of hope, a guiding hand.

Spirals of New Beginnings

In every heartbeat, life unfolds,
Spirals weave tales yet untold.
Through winding paths, we draw our breath,
In echoes of life, we taste the depth.

With courage raised, we break the mold,
In endless turns, our dreams are bold.
The dawn awakens, skies are bright,
New beginnings bathed in light.

Through trials faced, we learn to grow,
In every twist, the essence flows.
Spirals dance in cosmic grace,
Each moment cherished, time embraced.

With every step, we forge a way,
Embracing change, we find our play.
Spirals of hope, we'll follow true,
In vibrant hues, our lives renew.

So here we stand, with hearts ablaze,
In cycles rich, we sing our praise.
With open minds, we shall ascend,
Spirals of new beginnings, friends.

Constellations of Tomorrow

In starlit skies, our dreams collide,
Constellations form, our hearts abide.
With every wish upon a star,
We reach for futures, near and far.

In cosmic dance, our spirits soar,
A tapestry of hopes in store.
Each star a pathway, shining bright,
Guiding us through the endless night.

Together we weave, in fate's embrace,
A galaxy of grace and space.
Constellations whisper tales of old,
Of love and courage, brave and bold.

With every sunrise, new paths are drawn,
In constellations, we find the dawn.
The universe sings a song of glee,
For tomorrow waits for you and me.

So trust the stars, let dreams ignite,
In constellations, we find our light.
With hope as our compass, we'll explore,
The endless wonders of evermore.

A Leap Towards Tomorrow

In the dawn's soft light, we embrace,
A step into the unknown, a fresh space.
With dreams like kites soaring high,
We reach for the sun, letting worries fly.

The whispers of hope stir our hearts,
Each leap a promise, where courage starts.
In the dance of the winds, we find our way,
Towards the horizon of a brand new day.

Fears melt away like morning dew,
As we forge ahead, discovering what's true.
With open hearts and spirits free,
We'll paint our futures, just wait and see.

Together we rise, hand in hand,
In the journey of life, we make our stand.
A leap towards tomorrow, bright and bold,
A tapestry of dreams yet untold.

With every heartbeat, we dare to explore,
Unlocking the treasures behind each door.
With faith as our anchor, we'll bravely go,
The possibilities endless, like rivers that flow.

Blossoming Dreams

In the garden of time, dreams take flight,
Like flowers that blossom in morning light.
Each petal unfurls with a whisper of grace,
A tapestry woven, our hopes we embrace.

Amidst vibrant colors, our wishes bloom,
In the stillness of night, they shatter the gloom.
With every heartbeat, they gather and spin,
A dance of the heart, where the soul found its kin.

Through shadows and storms, they refuse to fade,
A testament to passion, in trust they are laid.
Seeds buried deep, in love's fertile ground,
Will rise from the silence, as joy shall be found.

Threads of connection weave us as one,
A symphony played as day meets the sun.
Together we'll nurture the dreams that ignite,
For the power of hope is our guiding light.

In the chorus of life, we'll sing and we'll soar,
With each bloom a promise, forevermore.
As dreams intertwine in a beautiful seam,
We'll cherish each moment, forever we'll dream.

The Hilltops of Hope

On the hilltops of hope, where visions reside,
We gather our dreams, and together we stride.
With the wind at our backs, and stars in our eyes,
Each step towards the summit, a treasured surprise.

The valleys may echo with whispers of doubt,
Yet in this bright haven, we dance and we shout.
For every hard struggle, a lesson we've learned,\nIn the warmth of our courage, our spirits have burned.

With hands joined as one, we face the ascent,
Turning trials to triumph, on visions we're bent.
With persistence our beacon, we'll reach for the sky,
And claim every dream as we soar on the high.

The beauty of life is etched in our smiles,
As we journey together through abundant miles.
On the hilltops of hope, we breathe in the light,
And cast away shadows, embracing our fight.

The vistas before us, wide and so clear,
Remind us of strength, of love, and of cheer.
As we stand on the peaks, with hearts open wide,
In the hilltops of hope, forever we'll bide.

Rising Tides of Courage

With the moon's gentle pull, the tides start to rise,
Awakening courage that never says bye.
In the ebb and the flow, we find our true might,
As waves of potential sweep us into the light.

Each drop of the ocean carries a dream,
Building up strength in a powerful stream.
With resilience as anchor, we push through the storm,
Transforming our fears into courage so warm.

As the waters may crash, we hold steady our ground,
For every resounding wave holds a sound.
It sings of our journeys, of battles we've fought,
In the moments of doubt, we find what we sought.

Together we rise, like a tide on the shore,
With hands clasped in unity, we vow to explore.
For the rising tides speak of strength and of grace,
Of finding our voice in this vast, sacred space.

With the tides of our courage, we learn to believe,
In the power within us, we dare to conceive.
As the ocean stretches wide, our spirits are free,
In the rising tides of courage, together we'll be.

Floating on Daylight

In the warmth of the sun's soft glow,
I rise like a feather, light and slow.
Clouds drift serenely in the azure sea,
Each moment a chance to simply be.

Waves of golden laughter echo near,
Whispers of dreams, so sweet and clear.
Suspended in joy, I dance and sway,
Floating on daylight, come what may.

The world below fades, a distant hum,
A place where worries can't dare to come.
With every heartbeat, hope takes flight,
In the embrace of the fading light.

Nature's canvas unfolds so bright,
Painting the sky with colors of light.
Each brushstroke sings of peace and grace,
In this gentle, infinite space.

As twilight drapes its soft veil down,
I wear the stars like a silken crown.
In a whisper, the day bids farewell,
Yet I remain, under joy's sweet spell.

Ascending the Heights of Aspirations

With every step, the summit calls,
A dream awaits beyond the walls.
Through valleys deep and shadows long,
I carry hope, my heart a song.

The path is steep, the air is thin,
But I press on, fueled from within.
Each challenge met, a lesson learned,
A fire ignites, a passion burned.

Rays of dawn break through the night,
Illuminating, guiding light.
I dare to climb, to reach so high,
Beyond the clouds, where eagles fly.

Atop the peak, the world unfolds,
A tapestry of stories told.
With every breath, I stand so bold,
Embracing visions yet untold.

In this moment, I feel so free,
Connected to all, to you, to me.
Together we rise, hand in hand,
Ascending dreams, a promised land.

The Dawn of Understanding

In silence blooms the morning light,
Awakening thoughts, so pure, so bright.
A canvas wide, where questions roam,
In search of wisdom, we find our home.

Through shadows past, the truth emerges,
With every heartbeat, our spirit surges.
The gentle whispers of the wise,
Invite us to see through clearer eyes.

Connections form in the stillness deep,
As stories woven begin to seep.
Each moment shared builds stronger ties,
Uncovering love through soft replies.

In the embrace of unity,
We learn that we all long to be.
Understanding dawns like morning dew,
Refreshing souls, old and new.

So let us gather, hearts entwined,
In the light of truth, we shall find.
A world transformed, where kindness reigns,
In the dawn of understanding, peace gains.

The Gradual Shift

A leaf turns gold as seasons change,
Transformations gentle, yet so strange.
Whispers of winds carry tales untold,
Of beginnings fresh and wonders bold.

Stars twinkle softly as night unfolds,
Hidden stories in silence hold.
With each heartbeat, a rhythm unfolds,
In the gradual shift, life beholds.

Mountains stand tall, yet they erode,
In time, even giants unload.
The rivers bend, the trees sway low,
All in harmony, the world in flow.

Each fleeting moment, a chance to grow,
Embracing change, we learn to sow.
New beginnings whisper their grace,
In the gradual shift, we find our place.

As dawn breaks anew, horizons gleam,
Inviting us into a vibrant dream.
Together we journey, in light we drift,
Hand in hand, through the gradual shift.

Serene Ascent

In whispers soft, the mountains rise,
Beneath the vast, unfolding skies.
A path of peace, where silence sings,
The heart takes flight on gentle wings.

Each step we climb, we breathe in grace,
A tranquil mind, a sacred space.
With every dawn, new light we find,
A journey shared, hearts intertwined.

The clouds drift past, in hues of gold,
As tales of strength and hope unfold.
Above the world, the spirit roams,
In heights where dreams can find their homes.

With every challenge, courage glows,
A steady pulse, the spirit flows.
Together stronger, we ascend,
On this serene path, without an end.

Sails Set for New Adventures

The horizon calls with whispers bright,
A canvas wide, in morning light.
With sails unfurled, we chase the breeze,
To distant shores, through restless seas.

Each wave a promise, every tide,
Leads us to where new dreams abide.
With laughter loud, and hearts so free,
We chart our course, just you and me.

The winds of change, they guide our way,
In vibrant hues, we greet the day.
With every gust, our spirits rise,
A symphony beneath the skies.

We'll sail through storms, we'll dance through rain,
Embracing joy, and facing pain.
With every star, a wish we cast,
For new adventures, unsurpassed.

Together we roam, hand in hand,
A tapestry of dreams, so grand.
With sails set high and hearts so bold,
A journey waiting to unfold.

Streams of Optimism

Through valleys green, the waters flow,
With hope and light, they gently glow.
Each ripple sings a song of cheer,
A reminder that joy is near.

With every bend, new paths appear,
In flowing streams, we conquer fear.
Reflecting skies in shades of blue,
Each drop a dream, each wave a clue.

The sun breaks through, the shadows lift,
In nature's grace, we find our gift.
With open hearts, we drink it in,
A chorus sweet, where life begins.

Let laughter dance upon the shore,
With every step, we crave for more.
These streams of hope, in motion wide,
In every heart, they gently bide.

So cast your worries, let them float,
In these warm currents, learn to gloat.
For in each stream, the future gleams,
A life alive with vibrant dreams.

The Flourish of Dreams

In gardens lush, the blossoms thrive,
Each color bright, the hopes alive.
With tender care, our spirits grow,
In every seed, a tale to sow.

The winds of change caress the leaves,
As whispered truths, the heart believes.
From roots deep set, we rise and twine,
A fragrant path, our lives entwine.

With every petal, stories spread,
Of daring dreams, where none have tread.
In sunlight's warmth, we find our place,
A world adorned with love and grace.

The seasons shift, yet still we stand,
In harmony, we join our hands.
Together strong, through storm or calm,
In every breath, we find our balm.

For dreams once sown are bound to bloom,
In vibrant hues, dispelling gloom.
With every heart, we nurture schemes,
In this, the flourish of our dreams.

Illuminated Journeys

In the quiet of the night, stars ignite,
Paths unfold, guiding dreams to take flight.
Whispers of hope in shadows so deep,
Each step a promise, in starlight we leap.

Wandering souls paint stories in the air,
With laughter and love, we shed every care.
Footprints in sand, like memories cast,
Together we forge bonds, forever to last.

Rivers of wisdom flow through our veins,
Echoes of purpose, breaking the chains.
With hearts wide open, we seek the unknown,
Illuminated paths, where kindness is sown.

In every heartbeat, the journey persists,
Through valleys of doubt, in love we exist.
With courage as our guide, we will not stray,
Illuminated journeys, lighting the way.

Ascendancy of the Heart

In the morning light, spirits arise,
Hearts beat boldly, reaching for the skies.
With dreams unfurling, like wings set to soar,
Together we rise, forever wanting more.

Within every struggle, strength we shall find,
Forging connections, where souls intertwine.
Hope blossoms bright, amid shadows we face,
In the dance of life, we find our true place.

As mountains we climb, each step becomes grace,
Embracing the journey, each moment we chase.
With laughter and tears, our stories unfold,
The ascendancy of hearts, a beauty untold.

Through trials and triumphs, love will endure,
A radiant fire, steadfast and pure.
Together we flourish, in unity's art,
The everlasting vow, the ascendancy of heart.

Transcending Storms

Amidst the tempest, we stand tall and brave,
Finding our strength, as the dark winds rave.
With hearts ignited, we dance through the rain,
In the eye of the storm, we conquer the pain.

Through lightning's flash and thunder's loud calls,
We gather our courage, as the darkness falls.
With each passing gust, we learn to embrace,
The power within, in the wildest of space.

As clouds begin parting, skies start to glow,
New colors emerging, from the pain that we know.
With every heartbeat, resilience we claim,
Transcending the storms, we rise up in flame.

Now standing firm, we look to the light,
Grateful for battles that sharpen our might.
The storm may shake, but we shall not break,
Transcending the winds, for our dreams' sake.

Boundless Faith

In the depths of our souls, where hope takes flight,
Breaks the dawn's promise, banishing night.
With hearts wide open, we trust and we share,
In boundless faith, we find strength in prayer.

As seasons may change and the paths may bend,
Through valleys of doubt, our spirits ascend.
With each whispered dream, a spark we ignite,
Boundless faith leads us, a radiant light.

In moments of silence, our hearts intertwine,
Building a fortress, where love will align.
Against tides of worry, together we stand,
Embracing the journey, hand in hand.

With visions unclouded, our futures will gleam,
In faith's gentle embrace, we will dare to dream.
So lift up your voices, let love be our guide,
Boundless faith carries us, always side by side.

Awakening Dawn

Golden rays break through the night,
Whispers of hope in soft daylight.
Shadows flee from the gentle glow,
A canvas fresh, where dreams may grow.

Birds begin their morning song,
Nature stirs, where we belong.
In every breath, a chance to start,
Embrace the world with open heart.

Mountains stand in silent grace,
Clouds drift slow, a tender space.
Time unwinds, the past now fades,
In the light, new strength invades.

Colors burst in vibrant play,
Chasing all the dark away.
Each moment ripe with possibility,
Awakening to what can be.

With courage found in every glance,
We dance upon this fresh romance.
Awakening, we find our way,
To greet the dawn of a new day.

Embrace of the New Light

The sun ascends with golden hue,
A world reborn, rich and new.
Glistening dew on leaves does shine,
Hearts awaken, yours and mine.

The air holds whispers soft and sweet,
Each moment feels like a heartbeat.
In shadows cast, the past does fade,
In this light, our fears allayed.

Hands reach out to skies so vast,
Together we rise, unchained, at last.
Lost in dreams, we float and glide,
In this glow, we turn the tide.

New beginnings gently unfold,
Stories waiting to be told.
In each sunrise, a promise waits,
An embrace that celebrates.

Let us gather, spirits bright,
Underneath the warming light.
A journey shared, side by side,
In this dawn, we take our stride.

Blooming After Storms

The storm has passed, the skies now clear,
Gentle breezes whisper near.
Petals open, colors bright,
The world reborn in morning light.

Each raindrop kissed the thirsty ground,
In every heart, hope is found.
Life emerges from the strife,
To celebrate the beauty of life.

Birds return to the swaying trees,
Singing songs upon the breeze.
With every bloom, a story thrives,
In the aftermath, the spirit drives.

Roots grow deep where once was pain,
From darkness, we begin again.
Resilient hearts, we rise and soar,
In the garden, we find our core.

Let us cherish this wondrous time,
In every moment, a chance to climb.
Blooming boldly, we stand strong,
Together in the joyous song.

Ascension of the Heart

Lifted high by hopes so bright,
Wings spread wide, embracing flight.
Through the trials, we found our way,
Ascending with each new day.

The mountain calls with a gentle urge,
To face the peaks, our spirits surge.
In the silence, we hear the call,
To rise above, to never fall.

With each beat, the heart defines,
A journey guided by love's signs.
In the vastness, our dreams unite,
In this ascension, hearts take flight.

Together, we reach for the stars,
Breaking free from all our scars.
In the light, our spirits blend,
With every step, we transcend.

Now we embrace the sky so wide,
In our hearts, no need to hide.
Ascension brings us strength anew,
With every heartbeat, we renew.

Glimmers of Tomorrow

In the hush of dawn's first light,
Flickers dance, a soft delight.
Hopes awaken, fears take flight,
Dreams emerge, a wondrous sight.

Stars that fade in morning's glow,
Promises of what we can sow.
Paths unfolding, visions flow,
Glimmers of the seeds we know.

Whispers of a brighter day,
Guiding us along the way.
Every shadow fades away,
In the warmth of sun's ballet.

With each step, new courage found,
In this space, we feel profound.
Hearts aligned, we are unbound,
Glimmers cheer in joyous sound.

As we chase what's yet to be,
Each moment holds a mystic key.
Together, strong, we'll journey free,
In glimmers, we shall truly see.

The Path to the Sunrise

A winding road beneath the trees,
Whispers carried on the breeze.
Footsteps echo, seeking ease,
Promises bloom like springtime seas.

Every shadow tells a tale,
Of those who walked before, set sail.
Dreams entwined on this grand trail,
Leading us where hopes prevail.

In the distance, colors burst,
Golden rays, a fearless thirst.
With each stride, we face the worst,
Yet in our hearts, the fire's first.

Mountains rise, we climb their height,
Together stronger, hearts ignite.
Towards the heavens, endless light,
The path reveals its pure delight.

And as the dawn breaks on the way,
Our spirits soar, no time to stay.
With every heartbeat, come what may,
We'll find our joy, the break of day.

Shattering Night's Veil

In darkness thick, where shadows creep,
Dreamers linger and secrets keep.
Yet hope's flicker dissolves the steep,
As dawn arrives from night's deep sleep.

Like a chorus, soft winds sigh,
Urging stars to say goodbye.
With vibrant strokes, the colors fly,
As the curtain of night passes by.

Each moment births a chance anew,
With golden rays, our spirits grew.
The world wakes up; it's fresh, it's true,
Shattering veils, we push on through.

From the ashes of yesterday's pain,
Resilience blooms, like summer rain.
Through trials faced, no soul in vain,
We rise again, our strength unchained.

As daylight spreads its wings so wide,
Dreams embraced, we'll no longer hide.
In unity, let's take that ride,
Shattering night's veil, side by side.

Blossoms of Tomorrow

In gardens where our hopes reside,
Seeds of dreams, the earth supplied.
With gentle hands, we nurture wide,
Blossoms of tomorrow, with joy and pride.

Every petal holds a sigh,
A story whispered, days gone by.
In colors bright, they catch the eye,
As time unfolds, and we comply.

With sunny days and rainy nights,
We tend the soil for future sights.
Through seasons' change, our heart ignites,
Blossoms bloom, reaching new heights.

In every bud, potential gleams,
A world reborn, the heart redeems.
Nature's canvas, a palette of dreams,
Blossoms emerge, or so it seems.

And as we watch the petals sway,
In gentle breezes, come what may,
Together, we'll embrace the play,
Blossoms of tomorrow lead the way.

A Tapestry of Possibilities

Threads of color intertwine,
A dance of hopes and dreams,
Each hue a story to tell,
In the loom of time it gleams.

Weaving moments, bold and bright,
A fabric rich with care,
Each stitch a chance to take flight,
In the tapestry we share.

Waves of laughter, tears unfold,
In patterns not yet seen,
The beauty of the brave and bold,
A journey yet serene.

Let the colors merge and blend,
With every breath we find,
A message that will never end,
Of love, both fierce and kind.

So hold this tapestry tight,
In hands both worn and warm,
For in its depths, there burns a light,
That transforms every storm.

Resilient Roots

Deep in the earth, they dwell strong,
A network vast and wise,
Through storms and droughts, they stand long,
In silence, they do rise.

Cracked soil cannot bear despair,
For life will find its way,
Through shadows cast, a growing flare,
Each dawn brings hope's bright ray.

Tentacles cling and twist around,
In search of light above,
With every pulse, a vibrant sound,
A song of strength and love.

From depths emerges vibrant green,
A testament of grit,
Resilient hearts and souls unseen,
Rise up where spirits sit.

Together, they defy the night,
In unity they bloom,
Through trials met, they claim the light,
In dark, they find their room.

From Darkness to the Expansive Sky

In the hush of night's embrace,
Stars begin to gleam,
Whispers trace the empty space,
Awake the slumbering dream.

Journey through the silent fear,
Where shadows softly roam,
Each heartbeat draws the dawn near,
A path that leads us home.

Through the veil, the light will break,
A canvas newly drawn,
With every step, the dawn we make,
A promise of the morn.

Embrace the vastness, let it in,
The sky is wide and clear,
From darkness blooms the flame within,
Together, we persevere.

From depths, we soar, hearts open wide,
With wings of dreams, we fly,
In unity, the world our guide,
As we greet the endless sky.

A Gentle Uprising

Whispers of change begin to swell,
In hearts that dare to rise,
A echo soft, a sacred bell,
That stirs the deepest sighs.

The dawn unfolds, a tender grace,
Awakening the weary,
With every voice, the world we pace,
In unity, we're cheery.

From ashes cold, we find our voice,
A song that warms the soul,
Through gentle steps, we claim our choice,
To let compassion roll.

With every hand that joins the cause,
A tapestry we weave,
In kindness grows a fierce applaud,
So many souls believe.

A gentle uprising, soft yet bright,
In every heart, it's sown,
We rise together, taking flight,
In love, we've always known.

Wings of Aspiration

In the sky, dreams take flight,
With hope's whisper, they ignite.
Soaring high, they break the night,
Finding strength in shared delight.

Each heartbeat fuels the climb,
A journey timeless, a dance sublime.
Through clouds of doubt, we dare to chase,
The light that calls us to embrace.

With every step, we rise anew,
What once was hidden comes into view.
Together, we carve the way,
Unfolding wings to greet the day.

In unity, we craft our fate,
In every challenge, we create.
Let aspirations lead us near,
Embracing all that we hold dear.

With open hearts, we greet the sun,
For in our dreams, we are all one.
With wings spread wide, we find our song,
In the wind, where we belong.

Echoes of Resilience

In storms we stand, though winds may roar,
With courage stacked, we face what's more.
Echoes of strength in every tear,
Resilience blooms, wiping out fear.

Through trials faced and battles fought,
In every lesson, wisdom taught.
With heavy hearts, we rise once more,
Finding hope at the core of the sore.

Falling down, yet we arise,
Painting colors across gray skies.
In unity, we build our ground,
Together stronger, hope unbound.

The past may linger, shadows cast,
But each step forward frees the fast.
With voices strong, we sing our fight,
Illuminating the darkest night.

Let echoes ring of what we've learned,
With every falter, passion burned.
In resilience, we find our way,
Together we'll conquer, come what may.

From Shadows to Radiance

In twilight's hush, the shadows dwell,
A whispered tale, a silent spell.
Yet deep within, the light resides,
A flicker bold that never hides.

Through the dark, our spirits glide,
Seeking warmth on hope's bright side.
Each step we take ignites the flame,
From shadows cast, we call our name.

With every dawn, the colors blend,
A canvas bright that will not end.
In unity, we rise and grow,
From every shadow, let light flow.

As petals unfurl in morning's grace,
We find our strength, our rightful place.
From shadows deep, we boldly stand,
Radiance blooms, hand in hand.

Together, we embrace the light,
Chasing dreams that take to flight.
With every heart, we weave the thread,
From shadows deep, our spirits led.

Gentle Comforts of Change

In the breeze of shifting days,
Change whispers softly in new ways.
With every pause, a chance to learn,
New paths reveal and brightly burn.

Through autumn leaves and winter's sigh,
We find the strength to let dreams fly.
In each goodbye, a new hello,
Gentle comforts in ebb and flow.

As flowers bloom with colors bright,
Change leads us into the light.
With open hearts, we greet the tide,
In every change, hope does abide.

From shadows past to futures vast,
We learn to treasure moments passed.
With every step, new roads unfold,
Gentle comforts, stories told.

So let us dance with each new phase,
Embracing life in all its ways.
For in the change, we find our place,
A journey sweet, a warm embrace.

Lanterns in the Dark

In the stillness of night, they glow,
Flickering whispers to guide the soul.
Each lantern holds dreams inside,
Casting shadows where secrets stroll.

Through the trees, a soft light weaves,
Mapping paths for wandering hearts.
In the quiet, courage breathes,
As hope ignites, and fear departs.

Beneath the stars, their dance unfolds,
A symphony of vivid hues.
They tell the tales of ages old,
In moments lost, they find the clues.

Though darkness wraps the world in veil,
These lights remind us we are brave.
With every flicker, love prevails,
And guides us over every wave.

In every heart, a lantern glows,
A beacon bright through stormy seas.
Together, we will find our flows,
As lanterns shine with gentle ease.

A Symphony of New Sight

When dawn breaks forth, the world awakes,
Colors bloom from shades of grey.
A symphony begins to play,
As light reveals what night forsakes.

With every note, the heart takes wing,
A dance of shadows lost in time.
Each scene unfolds, a verse in rhyme,
As nature's choir begins to sing.

In harmony, the flowers sway,
Their petals whisper tales of cheer.
In every breeze, a voice sincere,
A message shared in morning's play.

The rivers hum, the mountains echo,
In vibrant fields, they intertwine.
Through every sight, the soul can shine,
New visions spark where rivers flow.

With eyes anew, we walk this earth,
Embracing all the world can show.
In each soft sigh, in every glow,
A symphony of life and worth.

The Unveiling of Radiance

In shadows deep, there lies a light,
A spark existing all alone.
Through trials faced, it has been grown,
A hidden gem comes into sight.

As dawn ascends, it starts to gleam,
Revealing hues of warmth and grace.
In every corner of this space,
Awakening the silent dream.

With gentle hands, we lift the veil,
To cast aside the doubts and fears.
In every heart, a song appears,
A melody in fragile scale.

The path ahead, once veiled in mist,
Now sparkles bright with endless chance.
Each step we take, a daring dance,
Embracing joy in every twist.

In radiant glow, we find our way,
Through woven threads of love and light.
The world transforms, our spirits bright,
As we unveil a brand new day.

The Sanguine Journey

With every heartbeat, life unfolds,
A journey painted with bold strokes.
Through highs and lows, the spirit pokes,
In vibrant tones, our story molds.

From whispered dreams to roaring flames,
We navigate through joy and pain.
Each lesson learned, a drop of rain,
That nourishes our souls' own claims.

In crimson hues, we chase the light,
Together weaving tales of hope.
With each embrace, we learn to cope,
In laughter shared and love's delight.

Through winding paths, our voices rise,
As one, we sing our hearts' desires.
In every glance, the spark ignites,
A symphony beneath the skies.

The sanguine journey leads us home,
With courage stitched into our seams.
In every moment, there are dreams,
Together, we will never roam.

Lifting Shadows Away

In the quiet of the night,
Dreams take flight, out of sight.
Whispers echo, soft and low,
Guiding hearts where they shall go.

With each breath, the night retreats,
In the dark, the light competes.
Stars begin to fade away,
Hope now breaks the dawn of day.

Shadows lifted, spirits rise,
Painting light across the skies.
Every moment swirling bright,
Chasing echoes of the night.

Wander paths where shadows played,
In the warmth, our fears allayed.
Hands united, strong and free,
Together, we will always be.

Let the dawn embrace our dreams,
Filling hearts with golden beams.
In this world, love's gentle sway,
Brings the light to guide our way.

The Promise of Sunlight

Here comes the day, so bold and bright,
Casting warmth with gentle light.
Each ray whispers a sweet decree,
Awakening life, wild and free.

The promise of sunlight we hold,
In gardens where blooms break the cold.
Nature stirs with vibrant song,
In this realm, we all belong.

Golden moments stretch and yawn,
Painting colors on the lawn.
Shadows fade, giving way,
To the magic of a new day.

Bright horizons call us near,
With open hearts, we shed our fear.
In the brilliance, we find our role,
Fulfilling visions deep in the soul.

In every sunrise, hope will reign,
With every dawn, we break the chain.
Together we will rise and sing,
Celebrating what the day will bring.

Navigating the Dawn

As the night begins to yield,
Promises of light concealed.
Softly, gently, day arrives,
In its glow, our spirit thrives.

Waves of amber fill the skies,
Unveiling dreams with hopeful sighs.
Each heartbeat, a map's embrace,
Guiding us to a brighter place.

With the dawn, our hearts awake,
Every step, the ground will shake.
On this journey, we will grow,
Navigating paths we sow.

Stars recede, their duty done,
In the embrace of the rising sun.
Moments valued, cherished, true,
As day unfolds, we are renewed.

Let the light be our command,
Guiding us with a steady hand.
In the dawning light we find,
The strength to leave the past behind.

Whispering Winds of Change

Through the trees, the whispers flow,
Carrying dreams in the winds' glow.
Change is near, with every breath,
In the shift, we find new depth.

Rustling leaves, a soft refrain,
Promises etched in the rain.
With each gust, doubts start to fade,
In the winds, our fears are laid.

The horizon beckons wide,
In the breeze, we cast aside.
Every moment holds a chance,
To embrace the winds and dance.

Voices rise, a chorus clear,
Calling forth all we hold dear.
In the change, we learn to trust,
Finding faith amidst the gust.

So let the winds of change arise,
Lift our spirits to the skies.
In the journey, we shall find,
A brighter world, with love defined.

Tides Turned at Dawn

The ocean whispers soft and low,
Where shadows blend with the golden glow.
Waves crash gently upon the shore,
As night surrenders, forevermore.

Seagulls soar on the morning breeze,
Carrying tales of far-off seas.
In this moment, all feels right,
With new beginnings bathed in light.

Shells glisten under the amber sun,
A chorus sings as day has begun.
The tides roll in, then roll away,
Painting dreams in the light of day.

Footprints linger upon the sand,
Each step guided by nature's hand.
The horizon stretches ever wide,
As hope awakens with the tide.

In the stillness, hearts will yearn,
For every dawn, how the tides turn.
A dance of time, so fluid, free,
The world reborn, just wait and see.

Rebirth in the Rustle of Leaves

In the forest, whispers abound,
Where life awakens from the ground.
Each leaf a story, brilliantly spun,
A cycle of change has just begun.

Golden hues in the autumn air,
Nature's palette, beyond compare.
Rustling gently, the branches sway,
Echoes of life in a vibrant play.

Beneath the boughs, shadows creep,
Cradling secrets that the woods keep.
In quiet moments, hearts will find,
The magic woven in the mind.

Raindrops fall and kiss the earth,
Each droplet sings of rebirth.
From barren branches, buds do break,
In every ending, new dreams wake.

Through trials faced in sun and rain,
Growth emerges from the pain.
The rustle of leaves, a gentle sigh,
Echoes of life, as time drifts by.

Glorious Ascension

With every step upon the climb,
Reaching higher, conquering time.
Peaks call out with a radiant smile,
As dreams awaken, though it takes a while.

Mountains rise to kiss the sky,
With hearts aflame, we aim to fly.
Each breath a promise, each turn divine,
The summit's glow, a fate entwined.

Winds of change caress the soul,
In pursuit of greatness, we feel whole.
The echoes of past whispers cheer,
In this moment, we draw near.

Stars align in the velvet night,
Guiding dreams to brilliant heights.
A glorious dance of fate and will,
With every heartbeat, we feel the thrill.

Hand in hand, we chase the dawn,
For on this journey, we are drawn.
Towards horizons that beckon bright,
In glorious ascension, we take flight.

When Dreams Take Flight

In the twilight, wishes rise,
Like paper lanterns in the skies.
Each thought a whisper, soft and light,
As magic stirs on this wondrous night.

With measured steps, we chase our dreams,
Crafting hopes with silver seams.
In vibrant colors, passions gleam,
As hearts ignite in a shared theme.

Clouds gather holding secrets rare,
While stardust lingers in the air.
On wings of courage, we must soar,
To capture life, forevermore.

The moonlight dances on our skins,
With each new dawn, the journey begins.
So we will rise, break through the night,
Embracing all when dreams take flight.

In the stillness of the night,
Hope takes shape, a feathered light.
The world awaits with open hearts,
As every dream in our souls imparts.

Echoes of the First Light

In the dawn's soft glow, shadows fade,
Whispers of night in silence laid.
Waves of gold stretch across the sky,
As the world awakens with a sigh.

Hope ignites in the morning breeze,
Carried softly through rustling trees.
Each heartbeat echoes the day's embrace,
Revealing beauty in time and space.

Glistening dew on the grass does gleam,
Nature awakens from slumbered dream.
Birds take flight in a symphony bright,
A testament forged in the first light.

Rays dance lightly on petals fair,
Spirits lift in the tender air.
The horizon blushes, with colors new,
A canvas painted in every hue.

Beneath the sky where shadows blend,
The songs of life, a vibrant trend.
Eager hearts, ready to ignite,
Echoes linger in the first light.

From Ashes to Blossoms

In the heart of ruin, hope begins,
From charred remains, a story spins.
Seeds of strength in the ashes lie,
Awaiting the warmth of the sun's high sigh.

Life breaks through in bursts of flame,
Resilience whispers, calling each name.
Petals unfurl from their hidden place,
A dance of rebirth, a gentle grace.

Carry the weight of yesteryear's pain,
For every loss, a lesson to gain.
Fingers reaching for the skies above,
In every challenge, discover love.

Through storms we wander, paths unclear,
Each step forward sheds doubt and fear.
With every blossom, our spirits rise,
A tapestry woven, a sweet surprise.

From ashes we rise, united and free,
Embracing the light, the harmony.
In the garden of life, find a way,
To bloom with courage, day after day.

The Breath of New Days

Morning whispers with a tender sigh,
Inviting dreams as the night says goodbye.
A canvas fresh with possibilities wide,
Embrace the dawn, let your spirit glide.

The sun kisses dewdrops, sparkling bright,
Chasing away the remnants of night.
Every heartbeat pulses with promise near,
Each breath a gift, as the world draws near.

With open arms, we welcome change,
Life unfolds in colors, vibrant and strange.
The past slips away like shadows fast,
A symphony played as moments cast.

Finding strength in the unknown's embrace,
A journey begins, each step we face.
In the breath of new days, we find our way,
With hope as our compass, guiding the play.

So rise and shine, let your spirit soar,
For every new day opens a door.
In the quiet moments, we'll find the key,
Unlock the brilliance of what can be.

Carving Tomorrow's Dreams

With hands of hope, we shape the clay,
Molding moments where shadows play.
Embark on journeys of vision wide,
In the heart of dreams, let ambition guide.

Each whisper of purpose, a chisel's kiss,
Crafting futures found in bliss.
The stones may crumble, the earth may shift,
Yet dreams take form, a precious gift.

Together we rise, against the tide,
In a world of chaos, we stand with pride.
Carving a path with passion and fire,
Each heartbeat fuels our deepest desire.

Through trials and tears, we forge ahead,
With every struggle, new dreams are bred.
In the sculpture of time, we find our voice,
In the silence of doubt, we make our choice.

So carve tomorrow with love and grace,
In the story of life, we find our place.
With every stroke of courage, we see,
The beauty that lies in the quest to be.

The Redefinition of Home

In the heart where laughter blooms,
Walls dissolve, and freedom looms.
A hearth of warmth, of love's embrace,
In whispered dreams, we find our place.

Through open doors, new paths unwind,
With every step, we redefine.
Not just a roof, but bonds that form,
In every storm, a shelter warm.

Vibrant gardens, laughter's grace,
Memories etched in every space.
With every heartbeat, every sigh,
Home is where our spirits fly.

In shared moments, time stands still,
Love's quiet strength, a sacred thrill.
Together we weave a tapestry,
In every thread, a legacy.

So here's to home, wherever it may be,
An ever-changing symphony.
In hearts united, souls entwined,
A haven found, a peace defined.

Renewed Vows to the Day

Each dawn awakens dreams anew,
With whispered hope and skies so blue.
The sun, a witness to our plight,
In golden rays, we find our light.

Promises made in morning's glow,
With every breath, we let love flow.
The world unfolds, a canvas bright,
In vibrant hues, we chase delight.

Moments linger, soft and sweet,
In simple joys, our hearts compete.
We dance through hours, hand in hand,
In unity, together we stand.

The whispers of the winds remind,
Of laughter's echoes, sweet and kind.
We pledge anew with every sigh,
To greet the day, to always try.

With every sunset, vows renew,
In twilight's glow, our love stays true.
For in each moment, come what may,
We celebrate this precious day.

A Garden of Possibilities

In the soil of dreams, we sow our seeds,
Nurturing visions, tending to needs.
Each bud unfurls with a whispered prayer,
In this garden, hope dances in air.

Colors blossom in vibrant array,
Petals unfold as night turns to day.
With every sunrise, new paths emerge,
In the gentle winds, our spirits surge.

Among the thorns, sweet blooms do thrive,
In adversity, we learn to strive.
The fragrance of growth, a soothing balm,
In nature's embrace, we find our calm.

A symphony of life in every hue,
Each moment precious, each lesson true.
Together we harvest dreams unbound,
In this sacred space, love can be found.

So plant your wishes in the fertile earth,
Water them gently, give them worth.
In this garden, possibilities grow,
A wonderland of life we sow.

The Jubilant Climb

With every step, the summit called,
Through trials faced, we stood enthralled.
In rugged paths, our spirits soar,
Each heartbeat echoes, wanting more.

The mountains rise, both bold and grand,
In nature's grip, we take our stand.
With steadfast hearts, we greet the heights,
Chasing horizons, igniting lights.

The air grows thin, but we press on,
With laughter shared, the weight is gone.
In unity, our burdens lift,
Each moment shared is our greatest gift.

The view unfolds, a canvas vast,
In tranquil silence, our fears are cast.
With every triumph, memories weave,
In the jubilant climb, we believe.

So raise your gaze to skies above,
In this ascent, find strength and love.
Together, we conquer, hand in hand,
The jubilant climb, together we stand.

Evoke the Day

In the dawn's soft embrace,
Whispers of light arise,
Chasing shadows away,
Breathing life to the skies.

Birds sing their sweet songs,
Melodies fill the air,
Hearts awaken anew,
Hope dances everywhere.

With each fleeting moment,
Time gently unfolds,
Painting dreams in motion,
A tale yet to be told.

The sun climbs higher still,
Warming the earth below,
Life unfolds its riches,
In the radiant glow.

As twilight draws closer,
Colors blend and sway,
In this timeless beauty,
We evoke the day.

The Dance of New Beginnings

In the hush of the morning,
Hope begins to sway,
Unfolding like petals,
In the light of day.

With each step we take,
Change fills the air,
The rhythm of promise,
In every heart's prayer.

Obstacles may linger,
Yet dreams rise and twirl,
Embracing the moment,
With a brave new world.

As we spin through the seasons,
United we create,
The dance of the daring,
A future we await.

Guided by our passions,
Together we will roam,
In the dance of beginnings,
We find our way home.

Through the Fog of Doubt

In shadows of uncertainty,
Questions start to creep,
Waves of hesitation,
Where silence starts to seep.

Yet within the stillness,
A flicker starts to glow,
With courage as our beacon,
We continue on the flow.

Each step may feel heavy,
As doubt clouds the way,
But hope whispers softly,
To trust and to stay.

Through the thickest fog,
A path begins to clear,
With wisdom as our guide,
We conquer every fear.

Embracing our journey,
With love as our shout,
We find our way forward,
Through the fog of doubt.

Embers of a Brighter Future

In the ashes of yesterday,
Hope flickers and glows,
A spark ignites within,
Where the river of promise flows.

With every heartbeat,
We fan the flames of change,
Transforming whispers of dreams,
Into visions that rearrange.

Through trials that we face,
We rise up like the sun,
With embers of courage,
Combustion has begun.

Together we will gather,
The light that shines anew,
Facing forward with strength,
As we pursue what's true.

With the dawn of tomorrow,
Brighter paths will unfold,
Embers of a future bright,
Are waiting to be told.

Eclipsing the Darkness

In shadows deep, the whispers sigh,
As stars ignite the velvet sky.
Each flicker dances, casting light,
A beacon bold in endless night.

Through veils of doubt, we find our way,
With hearts ablaze, we chose to stay.
Together strong, we rise anew,
Transforming dark to vibrant hue.

With every step, we break the chain,
In unity, we feel no pain.
The past may haunt, but hope prevails,
Our spirit shines, the shadow fails.

In twilight's grip, we stand as one,
Embracing change, the battle won.
Through loss and strife, our souls expand,
A brighter dawn at our command.

Unbreakable Promises

In whispered vows, we find our truth,
Like roots entwined, we share our youth.
These bonds we weave, forever strong,
In every heart, we truly belong.

Through storms that rage and winds that blow,
We hold our ground, let courage grow.
A promise kept, a light revealed,
In darkest times, our fates are sealed.

With every tear, our love renews,
In joyful moments, we find our muse.
The threads of fate, a timeless thread,
With every smile, our fears are shed.

In silence shared and laughter bright,
We journey forth, hearts full of light.
Unbreakable, our dreams will soar,
Together now, forevermore.

Valleys of Serenity

In tranquil lands where silence reigns,
The gentle breeze, a sweet refrain.
Where mountains stand with wisdom grand,
And streams of peace caress the sand.

Beneath the trees, in shades of green,
We ponder dreams, both seen and unseen.
With every step on nature's path,
The burdens lift, we find our laugh.

The echoes of forgotten fears,
In soft embrace, they disappear.
In valleys wide, our spirits blend,
Where time stands still, and hearts can mend.

With every sunrise, hope ignites,
A canvas painted with pure delights.
In stillness found, we bloom and grow,
In valleys deep, our love will flow.

Embracing Radiant Change

With open arms, we greet the new,
The world alive with vibrant hue.
Through doors unbarred, we venture forth,
Exploring depths of unknown worth.

In every challenge, strength we find,
A lifting spirit, an open mind.
With curious hearts, we chase the light,
Embracing change, igniting bright.

The winds of fate may push and pull,
Yet in our dreams, we feel so full.
With every turn, horizons shift,
In bold embrace, we find our gift.

From shadows past, we shed our skin,
Awakening to the joys within.
With every breath, the moment's ours,
In radiant change, we bloom like flowers.

Canvas of the Unseen

In shadows deep, the colors blend,
With every stroke, the dreams extend.
The silent whispers paint the night,
In hues of hope, a hidden light.

The brush it dances, soft and free,
Creating worlds that eyes can't see.
Each point of color, life ignites,
Revealing truth in endless sights.

From storms that rage to calms so still,
The canvas holds both doom and thrill.
It speaks of tales long left to tell,
In vibrant strokes, we weave our spell.

With every flaw, a story spun,
The unseen beauty can be done.
Embrace the chaos, let it flow,
For art is life, and life's aglow.

In the gallery of the night,
Our dreams we paint with pure delight.
The unseen canvas, vast and wide,
Holds the secrets we confide.

The Dance of the Daring

Underneath the starlit sky,
Daring hearts come forth to fly.
With every leap, they embrace fear,
In the rhythm of dreams, they'll steer.

With courage strong, they break the mold,
A dance that tells of bravery bold.
Each twirl and spin, a chance to rise,
In the face of doubt, they touch the skies.

The music swells, the night alive,
Together they move, together they strive.
In every glance, a spark of fire,
Fueling the hearts with fierce desire.

In the shadows, where dreams hide,
Dancers find their truest guide.
With every step, the story's spun,
In the dance of the daring, they have won.

So let them sway beneath the moon,
In harmony, they'll find their tune.
For daring hearts who choose to soar,
In life's grand dance, they'll dance forevermore.

Threads of Resilience

In woven strands of tales untold,
Resilience shines, both brave and bold.
Each thread a story, woven tight,
In fabric rich, we find our light.

Through trials faced and battles fought,
In every knot, a lesson caught.
The tapestry of life extends,
Embracing all, it bends but never ends.

With colors bright, we stitch our fears,
With love and laughter, joy appears.
In every tear, a chance to mend,
The threads may fray, but will not end.

For in the weave, we find our grace,
Together strong, we face the race.
In every strand, hope intertwines,
Creating strength in fragile lines.

So let us cherish each small weave,
And in our hearts, we'll always believe.
For threads of resilience, strong and true,
Will guide us through the darkest blue.

A Cascade of Color

A rainbow spills across the sky,
In every hue, our spirits fly.
From gentle pastels to bold design,
A cascade of color, truly divine.

The sun dips low, the day transforms,
With every shade, the magic warms.
From dawn's soft blush to twilight's hue,
A symphony of colors, ever true.

In nature's brush, the palette glows,
Each vivid stroke, the beauty shows.
With every petal, leaf, and tree,
A cascade of color, wild and free.

In moments fleeting, colors blend,
As day gives way, and night ascends.
With every glance, a joy we find,
In every shade, the world's designed.

So let the colors paint our days,
In joyous bursts and gentle ways.
For in this life, a grand tableau,
A cascade of color, endless flow.

A Pathway to Tomorrow

With every step, the future calls,
A whispered dream that softly falls.
The morning light begins to break,
Each heartbeat sings for hope's sweet sake.

The road ahead is paved with grace,
Through shadows deep, we find our place.
Beneath the sky, we chase our sighs,
As stars ignite in velvet skies.

Together we will forge our fate,
With courage strong, we won't be late.
The dawn unfolds a canvas wide,
Our visions bloom, no need to hide.

The winds of change whisper so clear,
Each moment lived, we hold so dear.
A pathway bright, where dreams converge,
In every step, our souls emerge.

United hearts, we tread as one,
In every battle, we have won.
With open eyes, we seek the truth,
A pathway born from timeless youth.

Shards of Starlight

In dark blue skies, the comets play,
A dance of light that finds its way.
Each twinkle holds a secret bright,
A glimpse of dreams in endless night.

The universe, a canvas vast,
With every spark, the shadows cast.
In silence deep, the stories weave,
A cosmic thread we dare believe.

Through astral winds, our spirits soar,
On fragments bright, we reach for more.
In starlit paths of ancient lore,
We grasp the hope that's worth the score.

Each radiant beam, a promise made,
In every glow, our fears allayed.
With eyes aglow, we find the light,
In shards of starlight, hearts unite.

So let us dance beneath the glow,
With every spark, our spirits grow.
In cosmic dreams, we intertwine,
In starlit realms, our souls align.

Breaking Through the Veil

A veil of mist, a world unknown,
Where echoes of the past have grown.
With trembling hands, we seek the dawn,
To rise anew, to move along.

Beyond the haze, the colors gleam,
In shadow's clutch, we dare to dream.
Through trials faced and lessons learned,
A spark ignites, our souls returned.

We pierce the fog with hearts of fire,
Breaking through walls to reach our desire.
The path unfolds with each brave stride,
In courage strong, we will abide.

So let the light of truth be clear,
As we confront each hidden fear.
From darkness comes our inner song,
In unity, we grow so strong.

With every breath, we shed the past,
Through shattered chains, our spirits blast.
Against the tide, we rise so free,
Breaking the veil, our spirits flee.

The Soul's Resurgence

Awakening from dormant dreams,
The whispering of gentle streams.
In quiet moments, shadows fade,
A vibrant dawn, the night betrayed.

The heart ignites with fervent flame,
A journey born, no past to blame.
In every pulse, a story told,
Of battles fought and truths of old.

The soul's resurgence, ever bright,
In every challenge, we find light.
With arms outstretched to grasp the sky,
In every tear, we'll learn to fly.

A symphony of life unfolds,
In every heartbeat, courage holds.
With eyes anew, we see the way,
Towards vibrant life, we leap and sway.

Together forged through fire's might,
The soul awakens to its right.
In love's embrace, we rise and sing,
The soul's resurgence, purest spring.

The First Step Forward

In shadows deep, a whisper starts,
A heart that beats with weary parts.
The road ahead, though steep and wide,
Calls out to dreams long set aside.

The morning sun ignites the sky,
With hope that soars, it dares to fly.
Each hesitant foot, though fraught with dread,
Brings forth a path where fears are shed.

With every step, the past fades fast,
A brighter future, shadows cast.
The courage found in every stride,
In unity, we move with pride.

The world awaits, its arms spread wide,
To guide us gently, side by side.
In every heartbeat, strength ignites,
A canvas fresh, of endless sights.

We forge ahead with spirits bright,
Transforming darkness into light.
With every breath, we claim our space,
Awakening the dreams we chase.

Chasing the Faintest Glimmers

In twilight's grace, the stars appear,
A shimmering dance, a call so near.
The night unfolds, a canvas bold,
Where secrets whispered, tales unfold.

Each glimmer bright, a hope ignites,
In shadowed corners, dreams take flight.
With open hearts, we seek the glow,
Embracing paths we long to know.

Through tangled woods and winding trails,
The faintest light, our heart prevails.
For in the dark, we learn to see,
The beauty held in mystery.

As dawn approaches, colors blend,
What once was lost, begins to mend.
We chase the moments, fleeting, rare,
In every heartbeat, love laid bare.

The glimmers fade, yet hope remains,
In whispers soft, our spirit gains.
Together we walk, hand in hand,
Chasing the dreams that light our land.

Awakening the Silent Echoes

In stillness wrapped, the echoes call,
A gentle sound, through shadows fall.
From depths concealed, the voices rise,
Awakening tales, forgotten ties.

With every pulse, the night resounds,
In quiet spaces, wisdom founds.
A symphony of whispers sweet,
Each note a journey, incomplete.

Through memories that softly blend,
We find the strength in what's been penned.
The silent hues begin to speak,
In colors bright, the strong, the weak.

With every breath, a story shared,
In unity, our voices bared.
The echoes linger, strong and bold,
Unfolding tales that yearn to be told.

Together we rise, in harmony,
Awakening dreams we long to see.
In silent echoes, hearts entwined,
A tapestry of truths, defined.

Moonlit Reflections

Beneath the moon, in silver beams,
The world transforms, alive with dreams.
Night whispers soft, a tranquil ease,
As shadows dance among the trees.

Reflections cast on waters clear,
In quiet moments, all is near.
The stillness holds the night's embrace,
A gentle pause, a sacred space.

Each ripple tells of times long past,
In mirrored depths, our souls are cast.
The moon above, a watchful guide,
Illuminating what's inside.

With every glance, the heart takes flight,
In moonlit paths, we chase the light.
Through fleeting hours, the night unfolds,
A symphony in silver, bold.

In whispered dreams and starlit sighs,
The world awakens, softly lies.
Together we find our way anew,
In moonlit reflections, me and you.

Beyond the Gloom

In shadows deep, where silence lies,
A flicker stirs, a whispered sigh.
The dawn will break, the night will fade,
Hope clings tight, unafraid.

The world turns bright, the colors bloom,
As hearts awaken, dispelling gloom.
With every step, a spark ignites,
In unity, we chase the lights.

Through tangled paths, we will tread,
With dreams alight, and spirits fed.
Together we rise, our spirits strong,
In harmony, we sing our song.

Let courage swell, let fears depart,
The dawn unfolds, a brand new start.
Embrace the warmth, let shadows flee,
We find our place, we learn to be.

So as the sun spills gold on ground,
We stand as one, together bound.
Beyond the gloom, our spirits soar,
In love and light, forevermore.

The Wings of Change

With whispered winds, the future calls,
A journey awaits, as doubt softly falls.
Embrace the shift, let fears subside,
Awaken your heart, let hope be your guide.

The skies emerge, so vast and wide,
With every moment, we shed our pride.
New paths await, with light enfolded,
Together we rise, our hearts emboldened.

Each flutter brings a brand new chance,
To dance with fate in a timeless trance.
We break the chains, we set our sights,
With open arms, we welcome heights.

The essence of change is here to stay,
In stillness found, we learn to play.
The winds of fortune shift and sway,
Together we forge a brighter way.

So take a leap, embrace the flight,
With wings outstretched, we soar to light.
In every change, a truth we find,
The beauty lies in an open mind.

A Chronicle of New Light

In pages worn, a tale unfolds,
Of dreams reborn, of hearts that hold.
A whisper flows through timeless art,
Each word a thread, a beating heart.

With every line, a story weaves,
The tapestry of hopes and leaves.
In shadows past, the light shall shine,
A chronicle of love, divine.

The dawn ignites, a fire anew,
With every breath, we break on through.
A journey shared, through thick and thin,
In unity, we find our kin.

The ink will spill, the pages gleam,
With every chapter, a vivid dream.
The light within calls us to rise,
A chronicle written in the skies.

So turn the page, let stories flow,
In every heart, a spark to grow.
Through trials faced, the strength we find,
A legacy sealed, forever aligned.

Unfolding Wings

In gentle dawn, our spirits wake,
With open hearts, new paths we take.
Like flowers bloom, we stretch and sway,
Unfolding wings, we greet the day.

The world awaits, so vast and bright,
With every leap, we touch the light.
As seasons change, we learn to fly,
Through storms we soar, we touch the sky.

With newfound strength, we chase the dreams,
In every heartbeat, a song redeems.
Together we'll dance, together we'll sing,
Boundless in spirit, unfolding wings.

The open air, it calls our name,
A journey shared, we'll not be tamed.
Through all we face, in love we trust,
With hearts set free, it's a must.

So here we stand, the world in view,
With every breath, we start anew.
Unfolding wings, we rise and sing,
In unity's embrace, love's offering.

A Tapestry of Tomorrow

In colors bright, the threads are spun,
Dreams and hopes in patterns run,
Woven tight through day and night,
A future crafted, bold and bright.

With every stitch, a story lies,
Of laughter, love, and silent cries,
Together woven, hand in hand,
Creating visions, rich and grand.

The loom of time spins ever fast,
Each moment fleeting, yet so vast,
Embrace the change, let go the fear,
For in this dance, our paths are clear.

As vibrant hues blend into one,
We rise anew with morning sun,
A shared humanity, we find our way,
In this tapestry, come what may.

So let us weave with every breath,
A legacy that conquers death,
In harmony, our fibers blend,
A tapestry that knows no end.

Seeds of Transformation

In quiet earth, the seeds are sown,
With whispers soft, their dreams are grown,
Through storms and sun, they seek the light,
Awakening spirits, ready for flight.

Roots dig deep in fertile ground,
A world of wonders waiting found,
Each tiny seed holds endless grace,
A journey long, a sacred space.

Through cracks of rock, they push and strive,
With every struggle, they come alive,
The hidden strength in each small form,
A promise held within the storm.

When blossoms bloom, the change is near,
In colors bold, they quell the fear,
Transforming life with vibrant glee,
The beauty found in just being free.

So tend the garden, watch it grow,
With love and patience, let it flow,
In every seed, a chance to learn,
For in transformation, we discern.

Threads of Brightness

With gentle hands, we weave anew,
Threads of brightness in every hue,
Carrying warmth, a hopeful start,
Binding together each beating heart.

In the fabric of our days, we find,
The stories shared, the ties that bind,
Looming visions of joy and care,
In this tapestry, love is our prayer.

Through laughter and tears, we stitch the seams,
Crafting a world of vibrant dreams,
The threads connect, they intertwine,
In unity, our fates align.

As dawn arrives, the colors gleam,
A chorus singing, a shared dream,
In every thread, a spark of light,
To guide us through the darkest night.

So let us celebrate, hand in hand,
The beauty found in this grand plan,
For in each thread, there lies a tale,
Of brightness woven, we shall not pale.

Clouds Parting for Clarity

Beneath the grey, the sun does peek,
A moment still, the silence speaks,
As shadows fade, the light breaks through,
Revealing worlds, both bold and new.

Clouds drift away, a gentle sigh,
Inviting dreams to soar and fly,
In clarity, our hearts align,
Embracing paths we thought divine.

The shadows linger but lose their power,
Each ray of hope becomes a flower,
In fields renewed, we find our grace,
Embracing change in every space.

As vision clears, our spirits rise,
In open skies, we learn to fly,
With every breath, a chance to see,
The beauty in life's tapestry.

So let us walk where light can lead,
And plant the seeds of every deed,
For in the dawn, our truth will gleam,
As clouds part ways for every dream.

Shades of Brilliance

In the twilight's gentle grace,
Colors dance in soft embrace.
Whispers of the stars above,
Paint the night with dreams of love.

Every shade tells a tale anew,
Crafted skies, a vibrant hue.
Golden rays break through the mist,
Moments wrapped in twilight's kiss.

From the dark, bright hopes emerge,
In their glow, our spirits surge.
Holding tight to every gleam,
Guided by a wistful dream.

In the palette, a story flows,
Each brushstroke, our heart's prose.
Relics of what we perceive,
Shades of brilliance we believe.

As daylight merges with the night,
Every hue sings of the light.
Together, together we stand tall,
Embracing beauty, embracing all.

Embracing the Unseen

In shadows where the secrets lie,
We find strength and reason why.
With every heartbeat, we explore,
The whispers of what lies in store.

Invisible threads bind us near,
Creating bonds we feel so clear.
Through silence, stories softly swell,
In hidden realms, our spirits dwell.

Eyes closed tight, we sense the sound,
Of silent echoes all around.
In stillness, we discover more,
The unseen world, an open door.

Through the mist of dreams we wade,
Finding beauty unafraid.
Embracing all that's yet to show,
In the dark, our spirits glow.

Together we delve into the night,
Where the unseen shines most bright.
With every breath, we hold the grace,
Of mysteries in their rightful place.

A Whisper of Tomorrow's Song

In the dawn's soft golden light,
A new day breaks, a hopeful sight.
With every step, we rise and dream,
Tomorrow's song, a flowing stream.

It dances lightly on the air,
Notes of promise everywhere.
Carried by the morning breeze,
Filling hearts with gentle ease.

With open arms, we greet the dawn,
Embracing moments, life goes on.
Each whisper weaves a tale so bright,
Guiding us towards the light.

In shadows long, it leaves a trace,
A fertile ground where dreams can race.
A symphony of hopes reborn,
Echoing from dusk till morn.

Every heartbeat sings along,
To the rhythm of tomorrow's song.
Together we shall rise and soar,
Holding tight and seeking more.

Propelling Forward

With every step, we break the bar,
Chasing dreams, we travel far.
Through the storms, we'll pave our way,
In the dawn of a brand new day.

Momentum builds, we feel the rush,
With every heartbeat, in the hush.
Boldly stepping, hearts ablaze,
Creating paths in countless ways.

Together we will reach the heights,
Conquering shadows, embracing lights.
The future calls, a distant shore,
With every breath, we yearn for more.

Unified, we rise and stand,
Chasing dreams, hand in hand.
With vision bright and purpose clear,
We'll conquer doubt, we'll persevere.

In the dance of time and space,
We find our rhythm, find our place.
Propelling forward, hearts in sync,
Together stronger than we think.

Rising Shores of Destiny

Upon the dawn where dreams arise,
The waves whisper tales of old,
Each grain a part of fate's design,
A story waiting to be told.

With every tide, a chance to grow,
The sands shift gently, yet they stand,
Life's journey flows like ocean's flow,
Guided by a steady hand.

Shimmering light on distant grounds,
Glimmers of hope in every crest,
Through storm and calm, the heart resounds,
In seeking out the very best.

As footprints mark the fleeting scene,
The waves retreat, yet still they call,
To rise anew, to dare, to dream,
Embracing both the rise and fall.

In every choice, in every breath,
The shores reveal what we can be,
A tapestry of life and death,
Emerging from the endless sea.

The Resilient Sun

In morning's light, a golden glow,
The sun ascends, a mighty force,
Through clouds and storms, it fights the low,
A beacon bright upon its course.

It warms the earth with tender care,
In every heart, ignites a flame,
With steadfast strength, it learns to bear,
The weight of night, of joy, of pain.

Each dawn a chance to rise once more,
To shine beyond what's come before,
The resilient sun, a constant guide,
In shadows deep, it will abide.

Through trials faced, it won't retreat,
With every setting, serves a sign,
That even when the day's complete,
The light remains, forever mine.

In every heart, in every soul,
The sun's embrace will always dwell,
Through night and day, we remain whole,
With wisdom birthed, in stories tell.

The Canvas of Possibility

On canvas vast, our dreams unfold,
Each stroke a wish, a vibrant hue,
In silent whispers, stories told,
Of paths that wait for me and you.

With colors rich, we paint our fate,
In bold and subtle, shades combined,
Through every line, we create,
A masterpiece of heart and mind.

In every drop, a life anew,
Possibilities dance in the light,
The artist seeks what's pure and true,
Bringing the shadowed dreams to sight.

With brush in hand, we claim our voice,
In every blend, a spark ignites,
The future waits; we make the choice,
To weave our stories, day and night.

The canvas waits, our dreams in flight,
Embracing all we long to see,
In shades of hope, in darkest night,
Together, we can truly be.

Unfolding Horizons

Beyond the hills, the horizon calls,
With promise wrapped in every ray,
In moments sweet, the tempest stalls,
As dawn unveils a brand new day.

The sky expands, a canvas bright,
Adventures wait in vast terrain,
With every step, we chase the light,
And rise above what once seemed plain.

Each peak we climb, each path we trace,
Reveals the beauty of the fight,
In every struggle, we find grace,
A blend of shadow, strength, and light.

As dreams take flight, they whisper low,
Of places far, of sights unseen,
With open hearts, we learn and grow,
Embracing all that lies between.

The horizon beckons, vast and true,
With arms wide open, we explore,
In every breath, a world anew,
Unfolding dreams forevermore.

A Glimmer in the Gloom

In shadows deep where whispers dwell,
A spark of light begins to swell.
Hope dances gently, soft and bright,
A glimmer shining through the night.

Through darkest hours, it weaves its way,
A promise of dawn at break of day.
With every heartbeat, dreams reside,
In the heart's chamber, none can hide.

It calls to those who've lost their way,
Reminding them that light can stay.
Amidst the sorrow, courage flows,
A glimmer waits where the heart knows.

In every tear, a lesson learned,
Through every scar, a spirit turned.
In the gloom, we find our strength,
A glimmer shines; it's the heart's length.

With arms extended, we embrace,
Our fears dissolve as we find grace.
In unity, we face the tomb,
And find our light, a glimmer in the gloom.

Wings of the Morning

The dawn awakes, the sky's aglow,
With hues of amber, soft and slow.
Birds take flight on wings of dreams,
Soaring high on whispered beams.

With every beat, they chase the sun,
Unfurling joy, the day's begun.
In the stillness, hope ignites,
As shadows flee, embracing lights.

Through fields of gold and skies of blue,
The morning sings, a song so true.
A dance of life in gentle sway,
Embracing all that comes our way.

Each flutter brings a tale untold,
Of futures bright and dreams bold.
In the breeze, a promise flows,
Wings of the morning, where love grows.

Awake, arise, let spirits soar,
In the light, we are evermore.
With open hearts, we greet the day,
On wings of morning, come what may.

Seeds of Tomorrow

In quiet soil, the dreams take root,
Small whispers stir in humble fruit.
Each tiny seed, a world concealed,
A promise blooms, its fate revealed.

With care and time, we water hope,
Through storms and sun, we learn to cope.
In patience lies the strength to grow,
The seeds of tomorrow, we sow and sow.

Where shadows fall, light finds a way,
Nurtured in darkness, they pave the day.
In every struggle, growth can show,
The beauty born from seeds we throw.

With each new dawn, the blossoms rise,
Painting the earth with vibrant skies.
In unity, our hearts will roam,
For the seeds we plant will lead us home.

In gardens vast, our hopes will sway,
Through winds of change, they'll find their way.
Together we grow, forever free,
Planting seeds of tomorrow, you and me.

Horizon's Embrace

Beyond the reach of night's cool hand,
Lies a horizon, vast and grand.
With open arms, it calls us near,
Embracing dreams that conquer fear.

In every color, fate entwines,
Where sun and earth, in splendor, shines.
Each step we take brings us closer still,
To the horizon, where hearts fulfill.

Through valleys deep and mountains high,
We journey forth, beneath the sky.
With every heartbeat, paths are traced,
As we chase our truths in horizon's embrace.

In twilight's glow, we share a glance,
The universe begins to dance.
In unity, we find a place,
Forever held in horizon's grace.

Let time unfold, let stories weave,
With every breath, we learn to believe.
Together we'll rise, no fears to face,
One with the world in horizon's embrace.

Milton Keynes UK
Ingram Content Group UK Ltd.
UKHW022119251124
451529UK00012B/612